Dear Parents:

Congratulations! Your child is taking the first steps on an exciting journey. The destination? Independent reading!

STEP INTO READING® will help your child get there. The program offers five steps to reading success. Each step includes fun stories and colorful art or photographs. In addition to original fiction and books with favorite characters, there are Step into Reading Non-Fiction Readers, Phonics Readers and Boxed Sets, Sticker Readers, and Comic Readers—a complete literacy program with something to interest every child.

W9-AIA-232

Learning to Read, Step by Step!

Ready to Read   Preschool–Kindergarten
• big type and easy words • rhyme and rhythm • picture clues
For children who know the alphabet and are eager to begin reading.

Reading with Help   Preschool–Grade 1
• basic vocabulary • short sentences • simple stories
For children who recognize familiar words and sound out new words with help.

Reading on Your Own   Grades 1–3
• engaging characters • easy-to-follow plots • popular topics
For children who are ready to read on their own.

Reading Paragraphs   Grades 2–3
• challenging vocabulary • short paragraphs • exciting stories
For newly independent readers who read simple sentences with confidence.

Ready for Chapters   Grades 2–4
• chapters • longer paragraphs • full-color art
For children who want to take the plunge into chapter books but still like colorful pictures.

STEP INTO READING® is designed to give every child a successful reading experience. The grade levels are only guides; children will progress through the steps at their own speed, developing confidence in their reading. The F&P Text Level on the back cover serves as another tool to help you choose the right book for your child.

Remember, a lifetime love of reading starts with a single step!

To Emily Easton
—K.K. and P.B.

To my artist, technician, scientist son Nasir.
Keep up your great works!
—F.M.

Text copyright © 2018 by Kathleen Krull and Paul Brewer
Cover art and interior illustrations copyright © 2018 by Frank Morrison

All rights reserved. Published in the United States by Random House Children's Books, a division of Penguin Random House LLC, New York. Originally published in different form in the United States by Crown Books for Young Readers, an imprint of Random House Children's Books, a division of Penguin Random House LLC, New York, in 2018.

Step into Reading, Random House, and the Random House colophon are registered trademarks of Penguin Random House LLC.

Visit us on the Web!
StepIntoReading.com
rhcbooks.com

Educators and librarians, for a variety of teaching tools, visit us at RHTeachersLibrarians.com

Library of Congress Cataloging-in-Publication Data is available upon request.
ISBN 978-0-593-12084-2 (trade) — ISBN 978-0-593-12085-9 (lib. bdg.)

Printed in the United States of America
10 9 8 7 6 5 4 3 2 1

This book has been officially leveled by using the F&P Text Level Gradient™ Leveling System.

STARSTRUCK

THE COSMIC JOURNEY OF NEIL deGRASSE TYSON

by Kathleen Krull and Paul Brewer
illustrated by Frank Morrison

Random House 🏠 New York

Our universe began
with what is called
the Big Bang.
After millions of years
of darkness,
stars exploded into being.
BOOM.

Zoom ahead almost 13.8 billion years.

The Hayden Planetarium ceiling glowed

with what seemed like millions of stars.

Nine-year-old Neil looked up

with wonder.

Out his window in the Bronx,

it looked like there were only

about twelve stars.

Was this a hoax, a joke?

He wasn't sure,

but when the lights

came on,

he was starstruck.

Neil started looking up
whenever he could.
Even though
he lived in
a building named Skyview,
his view of the night sky
wasn't very good.
Bright city lights
got in the way.
So Neil used
his friend's binoculars
to study the moon
over the Hudson River.
"And it came alive,"
he marveled.

On a family trip out of the city,
away from all the lights,
Neil got his first glimpse
at a real sky full of stars.
It looked just like the
night sky at the planetarium!
Neil was hooked.

He now wanted to be

a scientist who studies

the universe—

an astrophysicist (AS-tro-FIZ-uh-sist).

Neil's parents weren't rich,
but they did everything they
could to help him.

For his twelfth birthday,
they bought him books about
space and a telescope.
His mind began to explode
with facts about the stars.

The more he learned,
the more he wanted to know.
To buy a bigger telescope,
Neil got a job walking dogs.

Neil went back to the roof
with his new telescope.
Some neighbors were scared.
Was his big telescope a rifle?
Was he an armed robber?

Sometimes they called the police.
When the officers arrived,
Neil showed them Saturn.
He used his favorite planet's
moons and beautiful rings
to make the police starstruck, too.

But at school Neil wasn't

always an "A" student.

And not every teacher was a fan.

He laughed too much.

And he spent more time

having fun than paying attention.

Then one teacher saw that

every single book report

Neil wrote was on astronomy.

She told him about classes
for young people
at his favorite place,
the Hayden Planetarium.
Neil was often the youngest
person there.
The classes were hard.
But he wouldn't quit.
Neil pushed himself to learn
more and more.

One day Neil got invited
on an amazing journey.
Many scientists and writers
were sailing to Africa
to view a rare solar eclipse.

At fourteen, Neil was
the youngest on board.
Working with the
experts made him feel
like a science superhero.

Neil's extra studying helped him get into the Bronx High School of Science. He won all the science fair prizes. But he also liked sports and dancing.

At fifteen, Neil went to
a summer astronomy camp
in the California desert.
There were scorpions,
spiders, and coyotes!

But he loved being at camp.
So far from city lights,
the stars dazzled him.
With his dog-walking money,
he'd bought a good camera
for taking sky pictures.

Neil shared those pictures
at his first public speech.
Being a teen
speaking to adults
did not scare him.
He was a natural!
Talking about science
was "like breathing."
And people liked
his explosive excitement.

Some people thought Neil should

focus on sports instead of science.

But Neil's love of space was like

a tank of rocket fuel inside him.

Every new fact he learned

added more fuel to that tank.

By the end of high school,

many scientists knew about Neil.

Even the famous astronomer

Carl Sagan wanted Neil

to come study at Cornell University,

where he was teaching.

On a snowy February day,

Sagan himself gave Neil a tour.

But Harvard was his final choice.

At Harvard University,
he kept stretching his brain
and his body,
keeping fit while
learning more
about the universe.

After eleven more years of study,
he earned the highest degree
possible in astrophysics.
He was truly one in a million.
A star.

Neil kept looking up,

learning and solving

cosmic mysteries.

Then at age 35,

he went to work at his

beloved Hayden Planetarium,

where his love of the stars had begun.

Within two years,

he became the head

of the planetarium.

Part of his job was

to go on TV

to share the latest

news about space.

He loved asking people,

"Have you heard this?"

In 2000, Neil and his fellow scientists decided that Pluto was no longer a planet.

The small, icy object was
now a dwarf planet.

Pluto lovers were upset.

But Neil showed that science can change
as new facts get discovered.

Today Neil deGrasse Tyson
is a rock star among scientists.
He loves to share what he knows.
And he wants everyone
to learn about science,
space, and the universe.

His hands wave

and his fingers snap

when he talks

because science is exciting.

Laughter bubbles up

because science is *fun*.

Neil has the power to

make everyone starstruck!

He'll never forget being

a small boy

having his mind blown

under a starry dome

at the Hayden Planetarium.

And whenever he goes outside,

he still looks up.

"Everyone should have
their mind blown
once a day."
—Neil deGrasse Tyson